the selected poems of
JENS AUGUST SCHADE

translated by
alexander taylor

curbstone press

These poems were originally published
in Danish by Gyldendal Forlag, Copenhagen.
Some of these translations first appeared
in POETRY NOW and TRANSLATION.

Cover drawing by Ellen Swift

Special thanks for support for this
publication to:
      The Augustinus Foundation
      The Connecticut Commission on the Arts
      The Danish Ministry of Culture
      The Eastern Connecticut State University
         Research Foundation

LC: 85-70040
ISBN: 0-915306-46-8
Danish ISBN: 87-7456-958-9

published by
CURBSTONE PRESS   Willimantic, CT   USA

the selected poems of
JENS AUGUST SCHADE

WOMAN

Of gold and fire are the feasts of my thought —
Why is your heart filled with anxiety?
Flowers are blossoming behind your breasts
you smell of apples and eternity

THE POET

Do you know the joyous poet Schade?
Have you seen him himself when the sun goes down?
There he sits on the edge
of the round globe, kissing his pencil.

Takes a piece of the sun —
and chews it in his mouth,
whistles a bit and presses on his heart,
. . . out of his heart fly the birds of the sun.

AT THE CAFE

A good song
a crazy little miracle
rolls out of the gramophone
while I grow silent.
And to the surprise of everyone
I push the chair out from under me
and go on sitting in the air.

Before me sits a girl
with ugly-looking teeth
and fickle eyes.
She grows silent.
—We know, we two,
what's going on inside each other,
and fierce as lions our souls kiss.

She rises into the air,
I with her,
we find each other
there above the table.
And to boomings and thunders of applause
over the miracle of the song
we coil ourselves around each other
and go carouselling out the door.

COPENHAGEN LIFE

I've heard trolley number 14
heads north early in the morning
I haven't seen it myself.
I've gotten up too late
my whole life long.

RAIN DIAMONDS

My heart — it's a frostwork window
the cold has created
I open it to the newborn morning
—blissful the sight, the smell

the black trees stand
they treasure century-old sights
they tint the winter-vague dawn
like daydreams

so many longings wakened
in soiled sleepy snow
it's sheer joy
to smell the breath of winter

I hear your dress
sliding like snow
I hear drifts on great plains

your footstep sighs
voluptuous kisses of earth —
we'll go far
we won't rest
we'll follow animal instincts
we'll go with them
be chased with the heavy clouds
sit with round houses about us
and keep the earth moving

it's just a painful need that needs to be
                                    satisfied
in the middle of the forest yours meets mine
and they collide in flashing fires
and grow tranquil

the rain diamonds drip and drip
in a morningdark winterwood

THE GODDESS AND THE POET

—The seething goddess
laughed at my heartfelt sigh . . .

She took my heart
and laid it in her lap —
with her loving fingers she cut it out happily.

And though I have to say it hurt me,
still it was a teasing and frightful happiness
to see how she ate it like Pippins.

And then when she had squandered me entirely
she took the golden bell of happiness from a cabinet
and put it in its place.

—Now I walk, poet and death's soldier,
tinkling with my heart . . .

THE GODDESS WANTS TO DIE
WITH HER POET

Listen, brother,
kill me —
I can't taste your wine anymore,
I don't care about your passion,
tuck away my shoes, keep them
as golden memories.

Then you can lie in bed
looking at the shining shoes
and say: there lay the goddess,
for whom life became far too bitter.

She relished it with ringing ears
and flaring nostrils —
she laughed when you made love, weeping
behind quivering eyelids.

Now she relishes the sight of the poet,
who is wasting away with desire,
now she wants to die in bed —
So. Listen, brother,
kill me.

THE GODDESS LONGING

Stars of silver and gold,
seductive apples
you placed in my lap —
but some day give me a huge warm heart
that can burn up between my hands
and moan and wail and sigh and laugh.
See my lips breathe and speak and thirst.
Let the soldier come to me,
—with cruel pleasure I'll coax out his heart.

THE OLD MOON AND
THE ETERNAL POET

Long have I felt you —
you phosphorescent moon,
the stars and the eternal
poet's victory over death.

I will hold out my heart
in a winged bowl —
and lift it high toward all of you like a little
warm and blinking lark.

Look at my heart send out its beams
it's like the ancient marvels
when Li-tai-pe took his dagger
and pierced the moon . . .

It bled . . . for he mistook the moon
for his own heart.

But Li-tai-pe's red blood
mixed with mine
and ran out through my hand's
beloved mystery
and placed itself on dead paper
as these verses.

—Here they sing toward the light
like the heart's tiny lark
and live eternally.

THE MARVELOUS VASE

The marvelous vase — with an eternal grasshopper,
which each day stands quietly in the same place
between darkgreen stalks. Behind it lies the moon
and a tiny dark temple. It's there I'd like to sit,
if I could sleep and lie down in the picture —
and watch the luminous beams from the moon on
                                    each tiny house
in the dark neighborhood. And hear the tones
from the vibrating grasshopper's immortal playing.

ME

Have you looked into my eyes?
It's a sight worth seeing:
There are midsummer nights
like lights in a mirror —
and lively women.

I don't know anyone
who looks like me.

I amuse myself
by going around observing myself.

What a mouth I have,
so large and sweet,
so light brown.

WULFILAS

The poor poet Wulfilas
alas doesn't have a dime,
hasn't had for quite some time —
ah how the world oppresses us.

The poor poet Wulfilas
didn't know whether to laugh or cry
so started chanting by and by
ah how the world oppresses us.

My necktie a bleached and crumpled mess,
I'm sitting on the top floor here.
I haven't enough for a single beer.
Ah how the world oppresses us.

But the sun travels in its round ring
each day around, in golden swing,
and the sun costs no one anything —
O, the world oppresses us.

And silverblue waves in morning light
stream toward us shivering white
singing psalms where life is bright —
O, the world oppresses us.

O could I kiss one single time
the girl who turned my life to rhyme
then I'd give a damn for morningsong.
O, how the world oppresses us.

Well, I sit here now with poetry
and neither food nor beer I see
and she doesn't give a damn for me —
Ah, how the world oppresses us.

NIGHT

Deep the vibration of the city
the fugitive heart
in a water-clear night
cooly luminous
the breathblue moonstone
of space

man's god-supporters
raise the black lines
say a desolate prayer
the world of the clouds moves off
cold eternal and lofty

SONG TO THE GODDESS

In the night's love writhing
I flung the fire flower of my soul
toward your smoking heart.

Laughter sounded —
and lying on a heavenly divan
you folded your hands around your neck
and drank from a blue cup.

It was heaven's cup —
filled with divine drink,
of flowing light from the moon
and sugarsweet heart's blood . . .

IN FRONT OF THE MIRROR

That white head in the mirror there has a body,
which is myself, which I now see shave
myself with my hand, which from the right side
comes into the mirror — I see glide

over these lips beloved laughter,
lips which smile glowingly in all the white
lather, which decks my stubble
of beard, turning me into an old geezer,

but when my white lather goes off
with the glide of the blade through these mountains
of snowclad glacial landscape — I see the veins
of springs from earth's interior stream

out of my face like the bright tears
which promise me the spring of Jens August Schade
with deep streams from my inner spring
which young and green lies behind the white hair.

EARLY MORNING

Beloved, soon the sun will rise
as we rise
rejoicing with the birds
over real life.
There is a wonderful darkness across the sky
(I remember this gray dark
through which my father and I walked when
                            I was younger,
in the gray winter morning,
and birds chirped faintly,
and trains whistled in the gray winter morning
in the lilac blue town
where I lived as a child.
And you walked beside us, beloved —
your smile was with me even then,
even though you had not been born yet,
and the stars gleamed like white celery down
                            from the sky —
from the pink hat
and down over your shoulders to your knee,
                        which was the moon,
whereas the sun was the pink hat
which rose behind the dark red walls
which were like lively lips
in the wet morning).
And now we arise in real life —
and you've become an "adult"
and can make a cup of coffee.

WE FOUND...

Hear the night birds scream,
now the gulls are there!
—hanging in the air, singing,
there are breakers,
the sea gargles
with round stones,
rolls and rattles,
white pearls
of white foam
purling around your throat,
queen of night!
Clean, raw, ripe, juicey
you stand in the sea, kiss me,
lie down between my arms,
joy keeps spraying in from the sea,
tumbles us around
like round pebbles
which meet and meet and meet —
two mouths, two people
among thousands of pebbles.
we found each other, mute,
among thousands of pebbles
and the world's stars.

JOY

In the early morning
we leaped up —
and walked among flowers,
it was spring,
birds flew
and sang in the trees,
there were dew-veils all over the meadows,
and our joy was like the bliss of heaven
while we still lived!
We laughed, we sang,
our mouths glistened
with our kisses.

I LOVE YOU

Round about me
the heavens spread in every direction.
I love you, you luminous space,
you long starnight,
spraying fire out of your innards,
and worlds ripen like apples on a mystic tree.

INGA

I love you like a lemonyellow ship
sailing over the sea, shining moon!
Sweet sigh! Almighty Inga Lyngbye,
life's power, life's wildness
in a little dress. Are you standing,
staring out to sea, gorgeous, your hair
spread out like gold in a round moon
about your head? Are you standing now
with nightwind whispering in your hair
spread out like a mirror of golden waves
under the moon, rising from the sea —
rising with clouds, which like your dress
wrap themselves around you — flutter lightly
under the moon — you walk quietly,
naked and spry under your dress, homeward
to your little house in moonshine,
across the earth's darkness, which is illumined by
your golden hair on Denmark's coast.

THE WOMAN BEHIND
STRIPES OF RAIN

Soft, delicate, calm friend
behind the numerous stripes of rain
over the numerous landscapes —
it's as if the numerous stripes of rain
contract into a thin curtain of painted
Chinese wooden pearls on strings,
a mysterious gray transfer-image
of those we possessed as children,
a veil of mist over something sensed
in the afternoon's thunder darkness —
and suddenly the landscape was there,
transferred plainly and clearly —
in all its luster of green and gold,
fields, woods, and distant clouds
and a gleaming lightning flash from the sky —
like when I saw you behind the curtain,
your golden knee and your ankle,
and a tiny stripe of your breast
darted down through your kimono.

ETERNAL VALUES

Even your stockings are timeless
when you have them on.
They have the stamp of eternity
and not merely eight dollars
seventy-five cents, Copenhague.
It's as if you weave them yourself
out of moonbeam glimmer
in your childbreast and your holy
adult breast — your blissful
walk on a moonbeam down
from the light behind the multi-national company
"Readymade Stars" to earth.
Behind your stockings' eight dollars
lies an eternity
as well as dew on a moonbeam meadow
with spider-spindle weaving
and dew in the morning-red rose.

MY BIRD OF LONGING

I lie in the night
almost unable to breathe,
something presses on my breast,
something — I don't know what it is —
then I heard a bird sing,
now I know it's my longing
which presses my heart a little,
so strangely, so softly
that it has suddenly opened
for my bird of longing
and now you no longer press on my heart,
lonely bird,
for now you are in it
singing tunes which lift it high
above loneliness
with you.

IN THE UNIVERSITY CAFE

Here sit I and Josefsen with long hair,
while streetlights around the world are lit.—
Here time and space disappear like coffee in a cup,
while life's evening leaves are slowly turned.

RAIN ON THE WINDOW

A mystical, fresh, mild spring rain
beats against my window, against Copenhagen —
the wind's cautious grip on the city
makes it tremble faintly,
touches something —
deep in my heart,
makes it tremble faintly
with all these windows, which sing
with the rain's drumming —
with happiness, which all these people got
through the rain at the same moment.

THE WORLD IS IN THE HANDS OF POWERFUL FORCES

The world is in the hands of powerful forces
that lift it and hold it in place
and sling it around on its course,
slowly or quickly, and cool the sun
or ignite its atomic explosions —
then we have winter all the year round,
polar dark and death's chill
throughout the whole, the whole year —
and not a flower, and you won't
be here with underpants under your dress
if these powerful forces want to cool off the sun.

And if it's hot, we'll have summer and spring
with swallows, trees, and chilled wine
in boats built tightly
from huge pine trees
and plunging necklines that reveal the breasts
of stately girls and women,
transitory, and yet not.

Absolutely not, for some are brisk
with death's dew upon them,
as well as the summer's nights, and really persist.
And autumn with warm winds and storms
in trees and reddish woods,
and pots of coffee, hot, and bread
and rain in the evening, mild and sweet
wine in the glasses, books, thoughts,
lights in the window, kisses moving like clouds
into each other — and flowers!
And winter with snow, and Christmas trees
and sparkling nights with snowflakes,
warm breath in the air
and ageless moonshine.

For we who love are full of fun,
we have no age, we are crazy!
We think we see joy in each other's eyes,
and hence we walk so joyously in the snow and spread
out our arms — and shout: "Hello!"
out into the winter night, we two —
we think it resounds in the wilderness
all the way over to the stars behind the park!
And over there at the store they certainly hear
our voices echoing from a flock of stars.
I wonder if they hear the least whisper
from the stars in back of their store counter? —

LET ME HAVE
A LITTLE RAINY WEATHER

Now the sky is so muddied with young stars
that no one can stay here in all the fire
no, let me have a little rainy weather on an earthly globe
of earthly spirit — where you can loosen belts
and ribbons pants dresses
and lie free — among all the dirt
with Your chemise on with its cloud-like lace
and unveil space under the quilts
so that one can sense the rotunda of your breasts
and the crowns of leafnets on your womb's
famous forests down there — a naughty
and strange word-notion has covered this
marvelous place for thousands of years
and no one could see how beautiful it was
in truly earthly fashion — a fresh rainy weather
in grass and roses is your soul's chemise
which covers the place — between your legs
and makes it beautiful. In transparency
of earthly spirit and rainy weather, pierced
by the sky's red morning sun so mild and strong,
all your cunt's sexuality is a creative work,
famous in the space where we have whored so often.

SHE SPEAKS OF THE NIGHT

Come beloved and kiss me long
up and down — with blissful heart
"Are you happy?" What do you think? Close
stars ring like chiming bells.

Look how small the universe is
in my arms. — It's as if You bring
bliss with You from where You come.

I don't know myself where I come from —
it isn't from the other side,
it's more like the other side
of the other side.

BORING INTO YOU

Boring into you
is like a delightful airplane
that lifts
on white wings
taking me with them
into the world of death
of deep roses
that sway fragrantly
wave peacefully
behind the raindrops of the stars.

AT THE MOVIES

We two criminals, who love to go to the movies,
while thousands are working with gas and confectionaries
and funnier things, income tax forms and the like,
we feel like gangsters and kings simultaneously
as we break the world's rules to pieces there
and sit blowing into each other's ears and doing
                              unreasonable things
in the theater — I look at the pictures
and touch your leg under your dress,
lay my hand on your arm and look up romantically at
                              the theater's heavens
while the pictures march past — and become strange,
supple, and do other things
while the world marches by up there on the screen,
close my eyes and think of other things, while they kiss
a soft movie-kiss up there, which touches
us deeply with its innocence, its pure nature
because it's a film. It's not a bit real,
they get a salary for it, earn money by it,
while we sit here carrying on, doing it right.
So you see we are criminals in a busy world, get
the grand inspiration from mechanical kisses
for a real production, home in our own
                    high-barbaric theater.

TRAVELING

A crowd of people arrive at a railway station,
they are so happy to be out taking a trip.
And we go over and drink a cup of hot, steaming coffee.
And the train with the locomotive in front
pulls away steaming into the hot morning.

Hot? Yes, chilly and cool and hot — it's a summer morning,
and the trees are wet and still glistening after
                                  the morning's dew.—
And the sun is red, rises fresh behind the railway tracks;
as fresh as your mouth was behind the steam of your coffee
it shines there in the smoke clouds of the train's stack.

Farther — farther — we come to Valby
where the morning doesn't bellow at all like the cows
                                  in the fresh dewfield,
but where the milkboys rattle cans and bottles, which
                                  the cows made,
and a young wife sticks her head out the window and shouts
                                  "More milk,
I want more milk up here on the fifth floor."

We come to Denmark's hovering clouds
so deep on the horizon. Gray and yellow
they rise up slowly. — Tiny little cows
stand far off, swinging their tails
and holding their shiny horns in the air like Vikings' foam
of seawhite froth about their helmet-clad brows!
A strip of sea has disappeared behind the peaceful cows.
                                  Now they are so big,
so close and munch. A farmyard rose
rises bursting from the earth in the gooseberry garden,
a bee comes humming lightly — and flies off again.

Now we're by the sea -- listen how the waves roar,

Now we're by the sea — listen how the waves roar,
blue, trembling with summer and sun, golden far out,
ships sway and rock fresh as fish
against the wave-splash, behind the hills' waving grain,
which trickles through a blue girl's fingers like water
                                    through a fisher's hand!

We sail on the ferry out into the blue,
again we drink a cup of coffee
so brown, so hot — so fresh, so wet is the air
in the chilly summer morning. The land lies so still.
Good morning, you gulls! Good morning!

WILD BERRIES

Wild berries in the shade of the woods —
who sows them? who watches them?
They have no nurse,
are simply there in the midst of heaven's riches.
Wild berries in the woods.

BY THE SEA

The sea is humming calmly, heavily:
Tulia, tulia, tul tul.
By the North Sea there's a pair of shoes.

The shoes are Karen's, both hide and hole,
they stand here now for a little while
as we have snuggled mouth to mouth.

And the sea rises in storms and night
from the North Sea to the Kattegat —
there where a tiny shoe was left.

And the breakers are roaring full of laughter:
now the sea fills the little hole.
Tulia, tulia, tul tul.

POETIC PIMPERY

I have a guest at my lonely table,
I, lord of my little kingdom,
—she sits before me, behind my bottle,
the fickle, blond girl.

With sourish wine I fill my glass —
life, it should be lived while high! —
I hear the moon-irradiated grass
fiddling about in the summernight's sigh.

She got drunk, too, tonight
and loves a peculiar master
who sits staring at her seat
while the world spins faster and faster.

My God, what's wrong with me? She's rising
from behind the bottle's cork,
it was the moon that sat with me,
holding the knife and fork.

THE SELECTED POEMS
OF JENS AUGUST SCHADE
has been printed in a
limited first edition
of 500 copies.

no. 116